NOT HERE TO STAY

Other books by Jesse A. Murray

Love or Baseball?

I Will Never Break

Never Found

NOT HERE TO STAY

A Poetry Collection

Jesse A. Murray

Off the Field Publishing
2021

Copyright © 2021 by Jesse A. Murray

First Paperback Edition Published 2021

All rights reserved. This book or any portion thereof may not be reproduced or used in any manner whatsoever without the express written permission of the publisher except for the use of brief quotations in a book review or scholarly journal.

First Printing: 2021

Paperback ISBN: 978-1-7751946-8-2
eBook ISBN: 978-1-7751946-9-9

Off the Field Publishing
Saskatoon, Saskatchewan, Canada

Off the Field
Publishing

Book design by Jesse A. Murray
Cover image: © Jesse A. Murray

This book is a work of fiction. Any reference to historical events, real companies, real people, or real places are used to make this completely made up story, a more believable experience for the reader. Other names, characters, places, and events are products of the author's imagination, and any resemblance to actual events or places or persons, living or dead, is entirely coincidental.

*For my Grandpa Senkowski.
Every time you pick up a guitar,
You bring a little bit of Nashville to Saskatoon.*

NOT HERE TO STAY

INTRODUCTION

How does one find the place where they belong? Well, I have come to realize that it's not about finding the place where you belong, it's about finding yourself. Once you find yourself, you can belong anywhere. But to find yourself, like anything else, you'll find yourself in the last place you look.

This poetry collection was written during a period of my life when my university career was coming to an end, and I was to begin my life in the "real world." I spent four months living in a small town in Alberta while I was completing my internship for teaching. I experienced what the country life was like for the first time, and I figured out that it wasn't for me.

After my internship, I was back in Saskatoon for a few months while I finished up school and earned my Education degree. But before I started my career as a teacher, I spent almost two months from July to September 2012 in Nashville, Tennessee. While I was in Nashville, I started to explore the idea of actually becoming a writer (as a profession and as an identity). Strangely enough, I was offered $50 to write a speech for a cab driver when I told him I was a writer. That would be the first and last amount of money I would make from writing for a long time. But that experience made me think that maybe I could pursue a career in writing. More importantly, in Nashville, I saw what was possible, and I saw what it was like for people that followed their dreams.

For over a year of my life, I was experiencing many new things, and going through a lot of changes. But most of all, I wasn't rooted in one place, and I felt the effects of knowing that where I ended up, I wouldn't be there for long.

When you end up in certain places, you get a feeling like you're not there to stay. Sometimes this could be a good thing, and sometimes this could be upsetting. With that said, when I wrote the following poems in this collection, I found myself in many different places, and I always knew that I wasn't there to stay. But each place had an important influence on my life and my writing. Looking back, it's clear that I was searching for my home, but I wasn't meant to find it yet.

This poetry collection is from writings that were written from March 10th, 2011 to December 28th, 2012. It also should be noted, that just like my first two poetry collections, the poems in the following collection are displayed in order from when they were written, and they are unchanged.

Jesse A. Murray
January 12, 2021

THE JOURNEY OF LIFE

Life is a million mile journey,
With a million different roads,
And how this life will go?
No one really knows.
But we keep on walking,
Just hoping to make it there,
We know there is a destination,
But we don't know where.
And when a million miles have passed,
And when we've travelled a million different roads,
One day the journey will end,
And we will never know.

THE WRITER

My mind is like whirlpool,
It takes everything in the world around,
Pulls it in, and sucks it down,
That is probably why other writers get depressed,
The world's problems become their own,
And so they never get to rest.

I have not reached this place,
But I can see how I could,
Maybe it doesn't matter, as long as the writing is good?

Should I let my mind become a black hole,
Should I let it consume itself,
To the point where I need help?

Or should I carefully tread the water,
And keep my head above the surface,
So I don't end up worthless?

But I could be worth a lot,
Maybe not in real life,
But by the words I write.

And so the writer doesn't matter,
Slowly he is falling apart,
But his words touch your heart,

And to the writer,
That's all that matters…

(…poets? Insane or sane?...)

THE WORDSMITH

He looks around the room,
As the shadows dance on the wall,
He is searching for inspiration,
He is looking for that spark.

It's that one thought,
That can engulf his mind,
And transfer from his hand,
Through the pen and onto the page
(And eventually to the reader's heart).

That one thought can ignite so quickly,
And it's tough to keep it under control,
Most people would be overcome by it,
But the poet is born for this.

The poet takes that thought,
He sets it ablaze,
When it's hot and malleable,
He forms it into his masterpiece.

He is the blacksmith of thoughts,
He is the wordsmith of words,
He is a master of his craft,
He is a poet.

NEVER MINE

Take my life and make it your own,
Take my mind and make it your home,
Take these words and do what you will,
Take these pages that I have taken the time to fill,
And make them last,
And make the past,
Live on, when I'm gone,
Forever.

THE WORLD KEEPS SPINNING

I'm at a standstill, but the world keeps spinning,
I keep losing, and they keep winning.
They keep moving forward, and I'm back at the beginning.
They try hard, but I try harder,
I go far, but they go farther.
No matter what I do, I remain hopeless,
But they don't even notice.
They are unaware, because they don't care.
And nothing matters, when you don't matter,
So I shatter the ladder, so I no longer have to try,
I will let any chance pass me by,
And I will let my dreams die.
I will become content with where I am,
Where I am at, and where I will always be,
Because nothing was meant for me.
No longer will I try to be somebody,
I will remain a nobody,
And that is the way it goes,
That just goes to show,
That we don't always reap what we sow.
But I do know that I'm at a standstill,
And the world keeps spinning,
I keep losing, and they keep winning…

(…I'm at a standstill but the world keeps spinning…)

FREE

…It's not the darkness that scares me,
It's the light, the ordinary reality of everyday life.
The obligations, the frustrations, and the awkward situations, that we are placed in. These are the things that are all around, and these are the things that bring me down. I just want to go back to the way it used to be…
…Free…

THE END OF PAST FRIENDS

…A part of me wants to take everyone I used to know, And just let them go once and for all. Because why do I think about the ones I never call? The ones that should be on my mind are the ones I talk to at the present time. I do understand that they were a part of who I was, but they are not a part of who I am, so I should stop trying to go back, and just leave what has failed to last, in the past. A part of me no longer wants to pretend, so this is the end of past friends…

FADING AWAY

…Good things come to those who wait,
But not to someone who is slowly fading away…

ANGEL TALKING

…I get pushed back,
It feels like I'm falling,
What the hell's that?
Sounds like an angel talking…

WISDOM

Wisdom is not knowing it all,
Wisdom is admitting you are unsure,
Wisdom is admitting that you do not have all the answers.
Wisdom comes with age,
Because when we are young,
We act like we know it all.
When we are young we are fools,
Because we do not acknowledge the fact,
That we don't have all the answers.
When we are young,
We do not ask for help.
When we are young,
We drowned in our own problems.
A wise man knows he can ask for help.
A wise man is not ashamed.
Wisdom is accepting the truth.
I accept the truth,
Therefore,
I am wise.

ILLUSION

Look inside my soul,
What do you see?
Peel back these layers,
Until you find the real me.

Read between the lines,
Listen to what is unsaid,
Hear what's in my heart,
And not what's in my head.

Let it flow through you,
Feel the word's meaning,
Let go of all your logic,
Read as if you're dreaming.

Use your intuition,
The first thing that comes to mind,
Do not think too hard,
There is nothing for you to find.

Everything is right in the open,
I am an open book,
These walls are just a distraction,
You do not even have to look.

I am just an illusion,
I fade into the mist,
Yet, you will feel my presence,
Even though I don't exist.

MORE TO YOU

Just let me go, push me out,
I am not someone you should think about.
Holding on to someone, just isn't fair,
Especially when there was nothing even there.
You created it all in your mind,
You remembered all the good things,
And left all the bad things behind.

Or do you see something inside of me,
That I cannot see?
Am I more to you,
Than I am to me?

Why would you want me around,
I would only bring you down.
What have I done for you?
I am not the one for you.

Just forget me, I think that's all I want.

(…Because I will never see you again…)

(…I feel like inside I am dying, I feel like stress is starting to take its toll, I must rejuvenate my soul…)

LOOKING OUT

…I'm on the inside and I am looking out,
Wondering what the hell this life is about…

ROCK BOTTOM

I have always been hard on myself,
my rock bottom would be success to everyone else.
At the top I'm alone, because no one else is around,
and since no one can reach me, I can only bring my own self down.
To myself, I'm the devil, I put myself through hell,
the only way I could be at their level, is if I fell.
I may be able to teach them the way to the top (level),
but in order for me to reach them, I'd have to drop (a level).

To others, my pain and suffering is glory,
it is no inspirational story. My low is a high, and
my high is unreachable, my dreams, unfeasible, my complaints,
unbelievable. But I will never be content, I will continue to push myself, even though my rock bottom is success to everyone else.

BAD DECISION

...A bad decision got you livin' through hell, You were close to heaven but in a split second you fell. The hard work was worth it, things were almost perfect, but old temptations crept in, leapt in, and you succumbed to it, even though it was dumb to do it. Now you have to suffer through it...

IN THE PRISON OF MY OWN MIND

…It feels like prison,
4 walls surround me,
And there is no hope to escape.

How did I end up locked up?
I swear that I am innocent,
I wish I could appeal the verdict.

Days are at a crawl,
There is nothing I can accomplish,
Every day is a wasted day.

There must be a reason I am here,
There must be something for me to do.
I must use my mind
(I must learn).

To learn, is my tunnel to freedom,
My mind got me here,
And my mind will set me free.

There will be a redemption against my mind…

(…My mind Redemption vs. Shawshank Redemption…)

INDEPENDENT VS. BEING ALONE

…She feels alone, her blonde hair lies flat on the pillow case, while she studies this stranger's face.
They met 3 years ago, they were once close,
But now it doesn't show.
She knew it would never last,
But he promised her, that this love would never pass.
Did he lie to her? Or is it her that changed?
Maybe he does still feel the same.
Yet, she has to leave him, no matter the cost,
There can be no love where a connection is lost.
At least that's what she tells herself, she needs to make her decisions on her own,
At least that's what she tells herself,
And she doesn't know that she was meant to be alone…
but she will…

PROBLEMS

…Blame me, hate me, I can take it when others can't, if you're stressed, get your problems off your chest, and throw them on my back…

DARKEST VALLEY

…I've seen the darkest valley, but only from the top, I've never been at the bottom, but I've visualized (pictured, been frightened of) the drop…

STANDOUT

…I have no idea how my life will pan out,
They see me as a standout,
Simply because I refuse to take a handout,
So I ran out,
It was time to find my own way,
I don't care what they say,
They will see some day,
That I needed to be free,
In order to be me,
Cause I will never win,
If I try to fit in,
That would be detrimental,
Because I wouldn't live up to my potential…

(…Break routine,
Escape route,
This is my journey to become a standout…)

NOT HERE TO STAY

...I just want to be heard, but the more you're heard the more money you make, but I'm not here to take, I don't want the money and fame, I just want to be great. And I'm not here to stay, I'm here to make a difference and then I'll fade away...

THE GHOST TOWN

Thinking of the town that no longer exists,
Once a place where memories were made,
Once held dear, but with time they fade.

Where are the people now,
Do they still hold a place in their heart?
Or like everything else, does it all just fall apart?

Now the town is just some nostalgic sadness,
That only a few feel,
But even to them the town is no longer real.

Even in their heart they are no longer the same,
They lost a lot of their life along the way,
And deep down they know it will all be gone someday.

Someone or something out there always takes your place,
Life just passes everybody by,
And the wind sweeps away all traces of you when you die.

But a thousand years from now,
There will be something that they will find,
Something in that town that you left behind.

The memory will be lost,
But there will be signs of the past,
And the town will forever last.

THE NEED TO BE WANTED

It would be a hard journey on my own,
But I guess it is for all of those who are alone.
We work so hard for personal gain,
Even if it causes us a lot of pain.
And we do this for one reason only,
That is, we are all afraid of being lonely.
We are all haunted,
By the need to feel wanted.
Being wanted is our motivation,
And it becomes our vocation.
It is what our life is all about,
It guides us thereabout.

But I wonder what happens when it is found,
Does it feel like your two feet are on solid ground?
Does everything fall into place,
A return to grace?

This is something we want to feel,
As if it can heal,
That yearning inside us all,
For once we can truly stand tall,
That feeling of really being alive,
For that is what we strive.

UNTIL I'M GONE

…My bags are packed,
I'm ready to move on,
I won't be able to change,
Until I'm gone.

No progress would be made,
If I chose to stay,
Trapped in my own hometown,
I needed to go away.

I wanted to change,
But I couldn't because of fear,
And this fear would last for as long,
As I chose to stay here.

So sad but true,
I'm a stranger in my own home,
A stranger to the ones that love me,
I've never felt so alone.

It's all in my mind,
I'm afraid to let them down,
And this fear,
Is the reason I am no longer around.

My bags are packed,
I'm ready to move on,
I won't be able to change,
Until I'm gone…

(...change will only happen when I'm finally out on my own. Until then, I can only prepare myself for the opportunity...)

FATE

…Sometimes I forget to let fate take a hold of my life…

FAKE MY WAY

…I take all that I know,
I fake my way through the show.
I make changes in order to grow,
I break routine and swim against the flow…

ONLY A COWARD

…Only a coward would stay
run away to follow your dreams
and they scream for you to stay
run away from their screams,
away.
Only a coward would
stay…

WHEN I SING

…I feel no pain, no love, no anything,
But when I sing,
I feel everything…

THE FORCE

…It's the force
that shakes the ground, and
you wait for
it to settle down…

A MEMORY

...Your footprints remain in the sand,
Where we used to walk hand-in-hand.
The ocean breeze,
Walking into the water up to our knees,
Feeling nothing but peace...

REMEMBERING THE DAY

...I remember the day when I wished you the best,
walked away, and I still feel pain in my chest.
God works in mysterious ways, he giveth and
he taketh away, and there is nothing I can do but pray. I can only wish to be happy again, I just don't know when the dream of us getting together again will end. I know it's hopeless, but the thought of you still makes me lose focus. You're not even the one that ended it, it was me, they say if you love somebody then you should set them free. But I know you will never come back, and I wish I could just leave it at that, but I can't and I won't, and I'm afraid I never will, and still I feel like I've got nothing but time to kill, until I fill this hole in my chest, as I remember the day I wished you the best...

>(...The unlived, unspoken, and unwritten word,
>will never be heard...)

NEED HELP

Do I need help?
I'll let my life speak for itself.
What have I got?

(…Do something about it, don't wait for it to come to you…)

TAKE ACTION

…Why are some people great?
Usually because they are willing to take action.
Yes, luck, being at the right place at the right time may be involved. But taking action is something they all have in common. When you take action, in a sense, you are going against the grain, since most people are unwilling to act.
Remember that…

LEGENDS NEVER DIE

…It lives in the earth and the sky,
I live my life as if I will never die…

…I don't speak of Wild Horses or Tumbling Dice, or No More Mister Nice. I speak of Strawberry Fields, Doors Of Perception, and Purple Haze. In other words the good old daze (days)? The legends that surround the ones who lived fast, and died young, the one who sung "she should have been a son."
The ones that failed to survive,
Yet they thrive, knowing they would never make it out of here alive…

…They live in the earth and the sky, legends never die…

I'M HERE AGAIN

…I'm here again, and until the end,
I learnt how to mend, adapt, and bend.
I no longer need anyone else,
I learnt how to help myself,
I no longer dwell on how I felt,
No turning back I have come too far,
It's not about who you were but who you are,
And now I see myself as a star…

GO OUT AND GET IT

…Nothing will come to me, I realize this now.
Anything I want, anything at all, I must go out and get it…
I repeat, nothing will come to me, nothing will come my way…
I must go out and get it…

SILENCE THESE VOICES

…And I said I would silence these voices that said that I would become nothing…And I became something…

BACK WHERE I STARTED

…For you, I have taken down these walls,
Only to put them back up again.
When you told me this had to end,
You said we still could be friends,
But I opened up myself to you,
Because you said you would help me through.
But now I'm back where I started,
Except now I'm worse off, and broken hearted…

DREAMS

…Life is way too short to give up on your dreams. To give up your dreams is like turning your back on your own life. Never bring yourself down. Never give up, because to give up, is to die. That's all I have to say for now…

(…I could sit and write forever…It is something I love to do…My dream…Write…)

A WRITER

…A writer can give meaning to things in this life that would go either unnoticed, misunderstood, or ignored. In a sense, a writer has the power to give meaning to life…

MOVE FORWARD

…When life takes a turn,
Go with it,
You never know where it will take you.

Some of the greatest moments of your life,
Might be just around the corner,
Turn that corner,
Find out what's there.

I see that turning back is impossible,
But that doesn't matter,
I see now that I never really wanted to go back,
I was just afraid to move forward,
But now I am ready…

(…I am no longer anything like who I was before…But that is alright, finally I am okay with that…I have a new life to live. I have my own life to live…)

SAT AND WAITED

...I sat and waited for that day,
Only to realize my life slipped away.
They say that patience is a virtue,
But it can also hurt you, in the long run.
Because you may die before you get done,
What you want to get done.

That's my biggest fear,
But as I sit here,
I realize I am making my biggest fear come true,
By sitting here, and not following through, with my plans,
And just like that, my life slips right through my hands...

...And it's my own damn fault...

QUIT SEARCHING

I need to give up,
I need to quit searching,
For too long,
This just hasn't been working.
I need to admit,
That I am meant to be alone,
No longer will I be in denial,
I will accept being on my own.
I will walk this path,
The ball always in my court,
I will accomplish many things,
Without any support.
I don't need anybody,
And nobody needs me,
All I need is to escape myself,
In order to be free.
I see it now,
It's all just a big change of plans,
And again everything ends,
Right back where it began.

I need to give up,
I need to quite searching,
For too long,
This just hasn't been working.

NOT THE SAME

I saw you yesterday,
But today is not the same,
We moved on so quickly,
We never saw it change.

I knew you for a day,
And you touched my heart.
I have no idea who you are,
But you tore me apart.

It doesn't even make sense,
But fate rarely does
I just know I wish I had,
The thing that once was.

ILLUISON OF PROGESS

…Simply taking action could bring you closer to happiness. Simply sitting back and doing what you've always done will keep you where you have always been. Learning and knowing without taking action is an illusion of progress. Progress can only happen when you take action…Remember that…

A JOURNEY TO BECOME A MAN

A shaky confidence,
With roots back to childhood,
But today I am doing things,
That I never thought I could.
I took the long road,
To get to where I am,
But after all these years,
I am back to where I began.
It's time for me to start a new journey,
To take another road,
But this time I am going to go,
Where I want to go.
I have wasted a lot of time,
So it seems,
But at least along the way,
I have resurfaced my dreams.
You see,
I got lost along the way,
I gave up on myself,
And worst of all,
I tried to be someone else.
But that was just not me,
It never felt right,
The things that really mattered,
Just faded from my sight.
But now things are in focus,
And I am seeing clear,
Now I can move on,
With nothing more to fear.

It has taken me to twenty-three,
But now I understand,
Today my life will begin,
Today I will be a man…

(…A boy can dream, but only a man can make those dreams come true…)

LONG ENOUGH

If I stare at it long enough,
It comes alive, it becomes real.
I can hear the waves crash upon the shore,
I can see the clouds move in the bright blue sky,
And I can feel the wind on my skin.
I was once there, a place that is thousands of miles away.
It is just a memory,
But if I stare at it long enough,
I can be there,
If I stare at it long enough,
I am there.

I MAY BE…

…I may be open or closed,
It all depends on what day you find me on,
I may be here, I may be gone.
I may be moving back, or moving on.
I may be weak, or I may be strong,
I may be silent, or singing a song.
I may be up, I may be down,
I may be flying, or on the solid ground.
I may be lost, I may be found,
I may be going forward, or back around…

PUSHED EVERYONE AWAY

…Now here I am, I have pushed everyone away,
There is nothing more for me to do,
There is nothing more for me to say.
I told myself "In order for me to be great, I need to escape."
And now that I am finally on my own,
I can't help but feeling alone.
Maybe I can't do this by myself,
Maybe I do need someone else.
I might be able to make it on my own,
But I need someone to share it with,
I found out that on your own, there is no such thing as happiness..

(…I may be able to push everyone away, but no matter what I accomplish on my own, I will never be happy alone…)

IN A CAGE

…It all started right here on a page,
When I locked my mind in a cage…

GHOSTS

I hear people calling me,
People I no longer see,
Ghosts of my memory,
From the person I used to be.
I no longer care,
Cause they're no longer here,
Life ain't fair,
For those unaware…

NASHVILLE, TENNESSEE

Now I was bound,
To a place I found,
Where I could for once be free,
It's that sound,
In this place,
Called Nashville, Tennessee,

That I have lived a dream of mine,
Even though I'm a thousand miles away,
I knew it would be my time,
But they've never listened to what I say.

And that's why I'm here,
All alone, on my own,
Face everything I fear,
But is there anything for me here?

HOW THINGS CAN BE

…For the first time,
I have seen,
All things around me.
No longer am I trying to be free.
I have felt trapped for so long,
There is so much that we haven't seen.

And this time at all cost,
I have been almost living an unforgiveable sin,
But I will always be around here,
No love we fear.

And for at least one day,
I have seen,
My life, my dreams,
And
How things can be…

WITHOUT YOU BY MY SIDE

I'm back on the road again,
A journey thousands of miles long,
I'm not looking to reach the end,
I'm not looking to move on.
I took everything I had,
And brought it here with me,
Even though it makes me sad,
I have to be free.

So I may break your heart
Yeah, the girl I left behind,
But it is your chance for a fresh start,
So push me out of your mind.

But now I feel reckless,
And I'm restless,
Without you by my side.

Without you by my side.

I want you to know, now,
I'm a hopeless sinner, and that,
I may be lost, but hopefully I'll be found,
But now I want to win her back.

But now I think sadly,
Will she even have me?
Or am I wasting my time?
How much should I leave behind?

I can no longer be there for you,
Cause I'm no longer around,
So you'll have to move on through,
Whenever you feel down.

But do not lose hope,
You will move on,
It's just a matter of time,
That you forget that I'm gone.

So take comfort in knowing,
That nothing lasts forever,
You won't ever remember,
That we were even together.

But now I'm so far away,
And a lot of time has passed,
And for once,
I'm no longer trying to make it last.

WITHOUT ME

Ain't nobody going to tell me
What to do tonight,
I'm going to do what makes
Me feel alright.
No regrets until the morning comes,
That's the way it's going to be,
It's about time
I start doing things for me…

I've heard this a thousand times before,
I can't keep living this way anymore,
Getting old is like a setting sun,
Each night a life is fading beyond a hill,
Like an old soul on the run,
But I can't worry about this now,
What is done is done,
Even though I wonder how,
I missed the starting gun.

Cause this life goes on without me,
Can you feel my pain?
You're no longer with me,
Can you see I'm going insane?

APART

my heart shatters
my life lost
no turning back
at all cost

no longer alive
dark
my heart
apart
my heart apart

WE WELCOME YOU

You make yourself at home,
We welcome you,
It's like you've been here forever,
What do you do?

TAKE A STEP BACK

Take a look around you now,
Where has it all gone?
Why do you feel so much pain,
When you move on?

Is it because you are lost,
For once in your life?
Did you realize the cost,
When you left that night?

I know some things are so hard to see,
When you are up close,
Take a step back from me,
To see what matters most.

Sometimes that's all it takes,
To see what's broken,
To fix the heart that breaks,
With words unspoken.

NO PURPOSE

Have you ever felt unwanted,
So helpless, and worthless,
You feel pain, cursed, and haunted,
With no destiny and no purpose?

GIVE IT MY ALL

And I sing my heart out for you,
Because I have the desire to,
Inspire the fire,
That's in each and every one of you.

So I give it my all,
Every time I write a word on a page,
Every time I pick up my guitar,
Every time I get on a stage.

I leave it all there for you,
My heart and my soul,
Now you know what to do,
To fill your own hole.

A CONTRADICTION

…I sit alone drinking,
Thinking, that I've been living a contradiction.
The more I mess up my life,
The better I write…

NO EMOTION

…And when I see your face,
My mind is filled with memories,
That I can't erase.
But when you show no emotion,
I can't tell what cards you are holdin',
Every hand I feel like foldin'…

FEELING GUILTY

…I'm finally feeling guilty,
But that's just the name of,
This bottle of wine,
I'm drinking…

LIVES ON THROUGH TIME

…This voice of mine,
Lives on through time,
By these words I write…

WHEN THE WHISKEY IS GONE

It's all happening,
It's all moving so fast.
Can I keep up?
Can I make it last?

But yeah, I'm back,
To be myself again,
And on the road,
The bottle,
Is my only friend…
But that's okay,
I'm never alone,
Except when the whiskey is gone…

…When the whiskey is gone…

NASHVILLE

Down in the streets,
There are those trying to make it,
And there are those in the office buildings,
Trying to fake it.
Some are young,
Some are old,
But all of them are bold,
They've followed their dream,
Escaped the cold

They are in Nashville now,
Gigging on music row,
They live day by day,
And have no plans for tomorrow.

These sorry souls,
These followers of dreams,
Today they have nowhere to go,
But the end may justify the means.

Cause being in the right place,
At the right time,
May reach someone's heart,
And someone's mind.

And that's what we sing for,
That's what we live for,
That's what we die for,
And that's what our dreams are for…

Someday we will see the light,
Someday we will climb the hill,
And maybe to the top,
In Nashville.

THESE FOUR WALLS (PART I)

…These four walls that surround me,
They try to drowned me,
They keep everyone out,
But they also pull me down.

But we do what we want to do,
These four walls,
Always judging,
Why I do, what I want to do,

And so many people tell you,
You can't do what you want to do,
But you do all you can,
To make it through.

Some say you will make it,
Some say you'll win,
Some say you'll lose.

…But now I'm on top of the world,
Just doing what I want to do,
Just making my dreams come true,
Come true…

(…But now I make my dreams come true, by just doing what I want to do…)

BACK AT THE BEGINNING

…But now we are back at the beginning,
Everything ends right where it began…

SO LITTLE TIME

I'll push you away
I'll block you out,
You're holding me back
I must get out.

I love this city,
It's still my home,
But there is so much world (out there)
That I could call my own.

So I must set forth,
On this journey of mine,
With so much to accomplish,
And so little time.

NASHVILLE THOUGHTS

…For the first time I don't want to leave,
For the first time I don't want to go away,
I finally feel at home,
Where I finally found a place I want to stay…

…I finally feel like I belong,
I finally feel like I found the place,
I was meant to be all along…

…Why do I have to leave (I don't want to leave),
But now I have to run back to something,
That I had to run from in the first place,
So much I wish I could erase…

…But now I feel lost,
More lost than I have ever been,
And I wonder if I'll ever win…

…I am living my dream,
But it is soon coming to an end,
And I don't know if I'll get this opportunity again.
I can't help but feeling down,
I can't help but feeling lost,
I want to stay here forever,
No matter the cost…

…I have to make a decision soon,
Before it's too late,
I finally found the place,
That I don't want to escape…

…I no longer have to pretend,
Here I feel I belong,
I should stay 'till the end,
But am I actually that strong?…

…To leave everything behind,
And go out on my own,
What am I to find,
Away from home?…

…Should I leave everything behind,
And break these chains,
Because without a dream,
What else remains?…

MY OWN ADVICE

…Some say if you dream it,
you can achieve it,
and some say take it,
or leave it.

And I say, follow your heart,
before this world tears
it apart.

That sounds nice,
but I can't follow my own advice.
That's why I regret,
a lot in my own life…

BORROWED SOUL

Some are here,
But gone tomorrow,
With a little bit of your soul,
That they have borrowed.

LEAVING

…I have never left,
Anything I didn't want to leave,
But now that I'm leaving you,
I can no longer breathe.
You have become a part of me,
You have entered my heart,
You have made my day,
But now you'll tear it apart.
I wish I could stay,
You were meant for me,
But I must go,
Into my misery…

HATE INTO LOVE

…Time will turn hate into love,
It will change things,
Just like it always does…

HOME

…I'm dazed and confused,
I don't know what to do,
I wonder if I'd be better off,
If I never met you.

I'm home now,
And it feels like I'm trapped again,
All opportunities are lost,
And all good things come to an end.

I feel like I took one step forward,
And two steps back,
But at least for a while,
I felt on track.

I have seen what was possible,
I have seen there is a life for me,
I finally found the place,
Where I can be free.

But what do I do now,
Now that I'm home,
Dreaming of that freedom I felt,
But now I'm all on my own?

When will I go back,
To a place I belong,
To the place I'm so far away from,
To a place I felt strong.

When will I see you again,
Or will I ever,
After a while will I forget?
How long will I remember?

Maybe time will pass,
And all will be lost,
Everything that was gained,
Will come at a cost.

Cause now I feel pain,
Now that I'm home,
And I'll keep feeling it,
As long as I try to hold on.

So maybe I must let go,
To that world so far away,
To that life that I loved,
To that place I wanted to stay.

I have touched my dreams,
Now I have to let them go,
Because all opportunities are lost,
Now that I'm home…

(…I have seen things, and have done things, that I have never done before, but now I'm right back to who I was before…)

A BOTTLE AND A GUN

…I've got black,
Inside my soul,
But that's perfect,
For Rock and Roll

I've got a bottle,
And I've got a gun,
Come on everybody,
Let's have some fun

I fired some shots,
In the air,
To see them run
And I don't care

I'm here to party,
I'm here to rock,
We're here all night,
We're never going to stop.

Raise your glass,
Drink it down,
Fill it back up,
With that Crown.

Keep on drinking
Let's raise the bar.
Drink 'till she's pretty,
Drink 'till he's a star.

We're here to have fun.
We're here to forget,
It's time to let loose,
With no regrets.

I've got black,
Inside my soul
But that's perfect
For Rock and Roll.

I've got a bottle
And I've got a gun,
Come on everybody,
Let's have some fun.

SWING FOR THE FENCES

…And my father said:

"If you swing for the fences,
If you take that risk,
Good things might happen, son,
You just might hit that home run…

HAD MY CHANCE

…It's my own damn fault,
I'm the one to blame,
I hold my own self back,
Now who am I to complain?...

…I had my chance,
But I didn't know it then,
This seems to happen,
Over and over again…

(…Looking back a lot closer now,
Maybe I did have a reason…bad timing?)

FELT THIS BEFORE

…I've felt this before,
But I can't remember when,
And I don't know,
When I will feel it again…

WHISKEY SUNRISE

We spent all night writing,
drinking, and having fun,
time seemed to fly by,
another whiskey sunrise.

Here's to the good times,
just another whiskey sunrise.

(...Our spirits seem to rise and fall with the sun...)

NOW OR NEVER

…Time is fading fast,
This won't last forever,
Let's try to make it last,
Since it's now or never…

I HATE IT HERE

I hate it here,
I cannot stay,
I hate it here,
I need to go away.
I hate it here,
There's nothing for me,
I hate it here,
I must go free.

Time goes by,
So it seems,
I stay back here,
I forget my dreams.

I waste away,
I fall apart,
I use my mind,
I ignore my heart.

This is my life,
It's all I have,
My heart, my soul,
Now it all goes bad.

No one sees me,
No one will,
I have been down,
At the bottom of the hill.

Time will tell,
Who really cares,
But that's okay,
Cause I'm gone from here.

FINALLY

I need to explain,
Why I left that day,
You must understand,
That this is not easy to say,
All I ask is that you listen,
To me:

…I've worked hard,
Only to fail,
I've pushed myself,
Only to lose…

…Life goes on without me,
I'm at a standstill,
I keep on climbing,
But I'm always at the bottom of the hill…

…We put on our masks,
Every day,
Wishing and hoping,
That we could fade away…

…Now that I'm here,
Far away from you,
I finally feel like I can do,
What I want to do.

Now that I'm free,
To live my life,
For the first time,
This feels right.

No more wasting time,
I feel things,
Will turn out fine…

(…Finally…)

MY DREAM

...You can take my soul,
But you'll never take my dream,
Away from me...

DON'T TELL ME

Don't tell me,
Don't tell me,
What to do,
No one knows me,
The way I do,
I've been here my whole life,
And not you,
So don't tell me,
Don't tell me,
What to do.

REVOLVING DOOR

I threw it all away,
I don't need it (you) anymore,
I need to put stop to this,
Revolving door.

You won't get back in,
Once you leave,
Boarding up these windows,
May make it hard to breathe.

But I need to stand strong,
Once and for all,
No more open doors,
I'm putting up a wall.

These four walls,
Will keep me safe,
Locking out these memories,
I plan to erase.

So just stay away,
I will never let you in,
It's about where I'm going,
And not where I've been.

This is my home,
You're not welcome anymore,
There are no more open windows,
And no revolving door.

WANT TO DIE YOUNG

I want to die young,
Before the damage is done.
I want to die young,
While this life is still fun.
I want to die young…

Right now I'm happy,
I have nothing more to gain,
I'm afraid the only thing left for me,
Is misery and pain.

I want your memory of me,
To be one with a smile on my face,
So I want to leave this life,
In a good place.

FOLLOW YOUR DREAM

Everyone is gone,
A stranger in strange times,
I see the past,
Within my mind.
I look in the mirror,
I no longer recognize what I see,
My eyes fill with fear,
I'm not who I'm supposed to be.

I go out in the world,
To live a life that's not mine,
Inside I'm dying,
But on the outside I'm fine.

This is for all of you,
That long to be free,
Listen to your heart,
And follow your dream.

THE GIRL I USED TO KNOW

I look at her now,
The girl I used to know,
I can't help but wonder,
Where did it all go?

From walking side by side,
Just yesterday,
To walking past each other,
Today.

Your eyes are distant,
What happened overnight,
Everything was perfect,
We've never had a fight.

But now you're gone,
Out of my life,
Out into the past,
And out of sight.

THIS IS MY LIFE

…I've been down,
I've been on top.
I've seen it all,
I've been through a lot.

This is my life,
It's the way it is,
It's the way it always will be…

DON'T LET HER GET AWAY

I looked in the mirror and said:

"Don't let her get away man,
don't let her get away…

"You've been searching for her,
for a lifetime, man,
you have to do whatever it
takes, to make her stay."

WITHOUT ME

Maybe it doesn't feel right,
Cause I'm wrong.
I go away,
Now you're gone.

I'm to blame,
No one else,
I feel pain,
Cause I'm by myself.

But I deserve it,
I was never worth it,
In the first place,

Just go on,
Without me,
Feel free
Without me,
Just be,
Without me.

I strung you along,
Maybe it doesn't feel right,
Cause I'm wrong,
I go away,
Now you're gone.

(…I can only blame myself.
I'm sorry to you, and
to me…)

TRAPPED

…I'm running away,
While I push you away…

…In prison, I'm in prison in this house, in this city, in my own mind…

…I will never be the person I want to be, while I'm still here…

…Trapped…

TOO LATE

Do you feel me now?
As you're alone,
My presence is felt,
More than before.

How do you explain that?
It's a mystery,
You feel me,
When I'm no longer around.

Time will tell,
So they say,
The truth lies within,
But you must wait.

You want me back,
But I would still be there,
If you kept me there,
In the first place.

Now

    you

        understand…

…Everything ends
Right back where
It began…

FINAL THOUGHTS

I wander off,
into the trees,
cool breeze,
shaking knees.

I felt this,
years ago,
the things I know,
seem to grow.

I become afraid,
of my soul,
becoming whole,
getting old.

I understand,
what I fear,
becoming clear,
the end is near.

AT THE BOTTOM OF THE HILL

...I'm not going back,
I'm not going forward,
I'm at a standstill,
 at
  the
   bottom
    of
     the
      hill...

STEP ON STAGE

The whole world,
Knows you now,
So step on stage,
And take a bow.

CROSS TO BEAR

She walks for miles and
gets nowhere,
just another lonely soul,
with a cross to bear.

SANG ALONG

…I sang along
And so did she
A little bit of my soul
Inside of me…

FOR THE LAST TIME

She sat on the floor,
With her knees in her arms,
Rocking back and forth,
Wondering how he could do her harm.

It started by yelling,
Fueled by drinking,
Then he hit her,
What the hell was he thinking?

She told him to leave,
He walked out the door,
He used to say he loved her,
But that doesn't matter anymore.

As the rain fell outside,
Tears streamed down her face,
She locked the door,
Just to feel safe.

It's happened way too many times,
She swore this was the last.
She hasn't seen him in years,
She left it all in the past.

PARADISE

As time goes by,
The ocean tide,
Will carry us away,
To a better place.
So we ride the waves,
As they rise and fall,
Flowing up and down,
Without a care at all.
This is the life,
Never felt so free,
Everything is beautiful,
As if it's meant to be.
So far away,
Yet everything is clear,
I am happy,
I love it here.

THE POET

It was written on the walls,
Down the empty halls
For no one else to see.

It was poetry,
But no one knew nothing of that then,
A life had to end,

Before anyone ever noticed,
So for a lifetime,
He was hopeless.

(...But he continued to do what he loved, while he was still alive. He believed in what he was doing. He loved what he was doing, and that is all that mattered. Now he is seen as a genius, even though he is no longer around...)

PULLING ME DOWN

…Pulling me down,
I can no longer breathe,
Why won't you let me leave?…

MORE THAN FRIENDS

We tried to be,
More than friends,
But I'm afraid,
This will have to end.

It doesn't feel right,
But it doesn't feel wrong.
Have I just been,
Lying to myself all along?

I think I'm not ready,
Not ready for you,
There's so much more,
I have to go and do.

I may be back,
Hopefully someday,
But I can't
Ask you to wait.
       But I know,
      By then it will be too late...

JUST WRITE

…Don't think just write,
Don't write just live,
Don't take just give,
Don't think just write…

THE COUNTRY LIFE

The country life,
The peaceful nights,
The poet's dream,
Was meant for me…

The crisp air,
The moon's glare.

CLOSE MY EYES

…I'm just going to close my eyes,
and let you slip away,
one last time…

GOING NOWHERE

She asked me where we were going,
And I said, "We're going nowhere,
That's the way it has to be,
We're going nowhere,
I have to set you free,
We're going nowhere,
It's time for you to see,
We're going nowhere,
You weren't meant for me,
We're going nowhere.

WAY TOO YOUNG

I'm here to tell the story,
Of how I let you down.
But first I'll say I'm sorry,
For never coming back around.

I was in over my head,
We were too much in love,
I was way too young then,
To give you enough.

JACK DANIELS

Do you know Jack?
The Lucky Number 7?
Have you met the man?
Do you know the brand?

All problems are erased,
With that charcoal taste.
Sometimes I wonder why,
That county is dry.

Then it finally hit me,
It must be the whiskey,
So I went to see,
This place in Tennessee.

I took the tour around,
I traveled up and down,
I've seen how it's made,
I've seen the highest grade.

I've tasted the single barrel,
I've smelt the sour mash,
It's all in my mind,
But it passes in a flash.

I wish I could go back,
That's my word,
The White Rabbit Saloon,
In Lynchburg.

So do you know Jack?
The old Lucky Number 7?
Have you met the man?
Do you know the brand?

I REGRET IT

I've never felt anything for you,
So I've tried to force it.
That wasn't right.
I don't know why I did it.

But I did,
And I regret it.
You deserved a lot more than I gave you,
And that's what I was afraid of.

I always thought I was never good enough,
But for some reason I tried,
Half-assed anyway.
I never gave you my all.

I knew it would never work out.
It was bound to fail from the start.
I coasted through life,
Never giving you any of my heart.

Did I string you along,
For too long?
I'll say I did,

And I'm sorry, so sorry,
But I did.

(...I realize now,
You can't love anybody,
When you don't,
Love yourself...)

THESE FOUR WALLS (PART II)

…Looking up and out to level ground,
When you're down, you're down,
So they say,
But maybe I like it this way.

I have a place to hide,
A place to cry,
A place to die,

And no one will ever know why.

Except these four walls…

SHE WONDERS WHY

She wonders why,
He doesn't come around,
She wonders why,
And can't help but feeling down.

Something so easy, shouldn't be so hard,
At least that's what she tells herself.
But what does she know,
Her experience can't be any help.
At least in this case,
When everything is different,
When the man she loves,
Is indignant,
And not a liar like the rest were,
Maybe that's why, this time,
She isn't sure,
But she forgets she never has been,
Not yet at least.

WINTER TIME

…The show, the road, the cold,
It's winter time…

ANOTHER SONG

…So I'm stuck here again,
With my paper and my pen.
I sit here writing another song,
Before these thoughts are gone…

STUMBLED

Looking back,
I have stumbled,
fell off the right path,
and into a long journey,
out of the way.

How do I get back now?

Do I turn back?
Circle around?
Or keep going forward
and make the best
out of my journey,
in the wrong direction?

Why couldn't I have
just stumbled,
and fallen into
a life that was
meant for me?

GROWING UP

Growing up on the other side of town,
I wish I knew a lot of things
that I know now…

…When I was left,
alone, at 8 years old,
in the cold, trying to find
my way back home…

YOU CAN BE HAPPY HERE

…I'm here to tell you,
Something you already know,
You can stay here,
You don't have to go.
You can be happy here,
You don't have to disappear…

SINGS HER BLUES AWAY

In the closet she has a box of old photographs,
They're the only things she has from the past.
She goes through them,
When she wants to look back,
On friends, family, and the good time she's had.
But every time they make her sad.
Cause she's so far away
From all of that.

But she's come so far,
Everyone now knows her name,
And leaving things behind is the price of fame.

So she puts it all back,
Into her shoe box,
And pours herself,
Another whiskey on the rocks.

She picks up her guitar,
And starts to play.
A tear falls down her face,
As she sings her blues away,
As she sings her blues away.

On nights like these,
She wonders what it would have been like,
If she stayed,
With friends and family,
And let her dreams fade.

WITH GOD ON MY SIDE

The devil takes my hand,
And leads me to hell,
For now until eternity,
This is where I'll dwell.

I've made too many mistakes
Throughout my life,
Now I have no more time,
To make it right.

I've lived my life,
But now I face the worst,
I've said for years,
That I've been cursed.

The devil has been watching me,
For quite some time,
He has stolen my soul,
And possessed my mind.

I can't give up,
Until I know I've tried,
But now I'm ready to fight,
With God on my side.

I'm no longer afraid,
I'm no longer afraid,
With God on my side.

STANDSTILL

…A step towards change,
can go a long way.
A standstill, however,
will always be a
standstill…

I SIT ALONE

…I sit alone on my bedroom
floor, trying to remember
all the things I don't have
in my life anymore…

A LITTLE SOMETHING

Everybody needs a little something,
To make the pain go away.
Everybody needs a little something,
To get them through the day.

PAIN AND GOLD

She was on top of the world,
but she was just a little girl…

…She takes a look to her left,
heart stops at the crossroad,
not knowing where she's been,
but she knows where she'll go.
That's the life she has chosen,
a life of pain and gold,
a life where she is forever young,
but she may get old.

Let go of the hearts of stone,
they will break,
or remain forever,
it doesn't matter,
if you're together,
she takes her soul
and goes with it,
picture perfect, picture perfect.

FROM ALL THAT REMAINS

In this state we will rise,
take all we know and survive,
no one knows our pain,
but we gain,
from all that remains,
from all that remains.

DEEP IN THE VALLEY

…Deep in the valley,
Away from everyone,
Deep in the valley,
Away from everyone…

THE WHISKEY

I've met Jim Beam,
I've met Jack,
I've met Crown, Black,
All on the rocks,
They've took me around the block,
I've seen it all,
They've seen me fall,

They've brought me up,
They've brought me down,
They've moved me on,
They've brought me around.

…From Canada,
To Kentucky,
To Tennessee,
It's the whiskey that carries me…

I feel at home,
Whenever I roam…

WELCOME TO MY SHOW

I was down yesterday,
And I'll be up tomorrow,
Welcome to my show.

Some will stay,
And some will go,
Welcome to my show,
Welcome to my show.

IT'S TIME TO MOVE ON

An old man sat at the bar,
Looking into his glass,
Thinking about his life,
Thinking about his past.

To everyone at the bar,
He was an old lonely man
With wrinkled skin,
But the reflection,
In the glass he was looking in,
Showed he was young again.

He said to himself, "Son,
The paint is chipped,
And the walls are cracked,
You can remember how it was,
But you can't go back,

They say time heals everything,
But it also changes everything,
Things get older with age,
So you must turn to a new page,

It's time to move on,
It's time to continue your story,
It's time to move on,
And forget about past glory.
It's time to move on,
And finally say you're sorry,
It's time to move on,
It's time to move."

He put his glass down,
It was now half full,
No longer half empty,
He walked out of that place,
For good,
He felt like he was twenty,
With his whole life now,
In front of him,

He said to himself, "Son,
The paint is chipped,
And the walls are cracked,
You can remember how it was,
But you can't go back,

They say time heals everything,
Things get older with age,
So you must turn to a new page,

It's time to move on,
It's time to continue your story,
It's time to move on,
And forget about past glory,
It's time to move on,
And finally say you're sorry,
It's time to move on."

RUN AWAY

Now that the damage is done,
And we had our fun,
It's time to run,

Run away,
It's time to escape,
Run away,
To a new place,
Run away,
Before it's too late,
Run away, run away.

LONG DRIVE

When you're feeling down
Go for a long drive at night,
On the ocean side of town.

SOUL

…I want you to shake,
rattle, and role,
and feel this music inside of
your soul…

…I want to tell you about something
I once felt,
a long time ago,
inside of my soul…

DEAR SELF

…I once found a letter I
wrote, it read:

"Dear self, what scares me the
most, is I don't need you
anymore."

I DO THIS FOR YOU

The air is cool,

The screams are loud,
The bottle kicks in,
It's time to rock the crowd.

You stand before the mic,
In this open field,
This is all a dream,
It does not seem real.

The band begins to play,
Exactly how you rehearsed that day,

It's time to let go,
It's time to sing out,

And the show begins…

This is my life,
I live on the stage,
It's just another show,
It's just another page,

I do this for you,
I do this for me,
As long as we're in this together,
For a night we'll be free.

And when the show ends,
We head out on the road,
We must do it again,
At the next show.

I'm with my friends,
But I miss my family,
Life is tough on the road,
It's wearing down on me.

But I must go on,
And the show begins…

This is my life,
I live on the stage,
It's not just another show,
It's not just another page.

I do this for you,
I do this for me,
As long as we're in this together,
For a night we'll be free.

I know this won't last forever,
But right now this is my life,
I do this for you,
I do this for me,
As long as we're in this together,
For a night we'll be free.

VACATION

I'm just here to relax.
I'm not thinking about anything,

I don't want to go back,

Cause I'm on vacation,
On the sunny side of the world,
And I don't care about anything,
It's just me and my girl.

GONE AGAIN

…In a hotel room tonight again,
the only place where you exist today,
and no one remembers you tomorrow…
gone again…

VEGAS

…At night in a strange world, I have walked and seen it all…I can be everywhere…nonexistent…

I WAS TOLD

…And I was told…in order for me to
turn it into gold…I had to reach
inside my soul…

About the Author

Jesse A. Murray is a Canadian author, poet, and high school teacher. He is most known for his debut novel *Love or Baseball?* (2018) and his two other poetry collections: *I Will Never Break* (2020) and *Never Found* (2021). He currently lives in Saskatoon, Saskatchewan.

Visit Jesseamurray.com for more information and current updates on Jesse's future projects.

www.ingramcontent.com/pod-product-compliance
Lightning Source LLC
Chambersburg PA
CBHW020916080526
44589CB00011B/620